HEAVEN

The Katharine Bakeless Nason Literary Publication Prizes

The Bakeless Literary Publication Prizes are sponsored by the Bread Loaf Writers' Conference of Middlebury College to support the publication of first books. The manuscripts are selected through an open competition and are published by University Press of New England/ Middlebury College Press.

Competition Winners in Poetry

1996
Mary Jo Bang, *Apology for Want*
JUDGE: Edward Hirsch

1997
m loncar, *66 galaxie*
JUDGE: Garret Hongo

1998
Chris Forhan, *Forgive Us Our Happiness*
Daniel Tobin, *Where the World Is Made*
JUDGE: Ellen Bryant Voigt

1999
Jill Alexander Essbaum, *Heaven*
JUDGE: Agha Shahid Ali

HEAVEN

Jill Alexander Essbaum

A Middlebury College / Bread Loaf Book

PUBLISHED BY UNIVERSITY PRESS OF NEW ENGLAND

HANOVER AND LONDON

Middlebury College Press

University Press of New England, Hanover, NH 03755

Printed in the United States of America

5 4 3 2 1

CIP data appear at the end of the book

. . . for Axel

Contents

Acknowledgments

I wish to express grateful acknowledgment to the editors of the following publications in which these poems first appeared, in one form or another: *The Listening Eye*, "The World to Come"; *Kinesis*, "The Dance of Salome"; *Rattle*, "Ararat"; *Wascana Review*, "Tongues of Fire"; *The Texas Observer*, "Untilling"; *Midwest Poetry Review*, "Eve at Noon"; *Rather-vue*, "Lullaby for a Good Friday" and "Equinox."

"Post-Communion Striptease," "In the Beginning," "When the Kingdom Comes," and "Paradise" appear in *The New American Poets: A Bread Loaf Anthology*.

"Easter" won the 1996 University of Texas Co-op poetry prize.

I would also like to express heartfelt thanks to the Michener Center for Writers, The University of Texas, and David Wevill, Thomas Whitbread, and Naomi Shihab Nye—three of the best readers anyone could ask for.

Deep gratitude to the Bread Loaf Writers' Conference and Agha Shahid Ali.

Special thanks to family and friends. I am truly blessed.

HEAVEN

In the Beginning

It was October once, fragile as
all autumn falling out, and God wept only
at dark windows, so that no one ever knew.

Then one evening sitting deep in the sky,
east enough to stay shadow in the setting sun,
God carved into the palms of God
and rivers bled from that magnificent wound.
They clotted into continents, and it was *good*.

But only for a little while.
You see, the twins, they came out crooked.
The first was king of shivering, and the second,
brilliant as madness, but far too comfortable
    at the hip and thigh.

This was good, but not *as good*, for he was always cold,
and she, warm as flesh and bedstead-soft.

They stayed that way for many years.

Evening

The sun, braggart
of light that it is,
has gone down,
hissing.

From behind the forbidden
tree, the man chews and begs
down the tips of his nails
until his fingers
are as naked as he is.

The woman—picture her
luscious and sly—cradles
the fruit in her breast
like the half-eaten head
of a lover.

Already he is off
to find the figs.

So she's going to bleed—
so what? She's sitting wide
as a grin, elbows on her knees,
leaning forward.

And her breasts depend on it,
two lovely dangling cherubs,
as she takes another
bite. It

is the sweetest apple ever.

Advent

The answer I seek is one I do not truly wish to know:
a useless unangelic laugh, *don't bother waiting up*
he isn't coming, as an even abject moon advises
learn to live without. And, as every year, I repeat
myself, wrapping figs and treats to give as gifts.

In waiting I learn to live with the anticipations of loss—
the sister arriving nine months on time but bloated,
not to survive, or no news from a telephone that will not ring,
these friends of mine who do not write, a God who won't relent.
Is it a perfect midnight I attend,

an evening flush with clouds and finally, *finally*
the man to whom I offer all my pain?
It is like this every year—a baby king
is born to die, and I will sleep alone,
failing at the very thing I fear failure of.

The snow makes night seem less significant
such that I am getting along fine these days.
But this peace we speak of God is hardly peace at all,
it is my cold, my terrified flesh, a physical fact
among other physical facts, and only that.

Oh Adam

It is not this apple I am hungry for:
I stay my breath, an honest moon above, and four
times four what I might ever bear of suffering—
I grieve you as a lover grieves, *lingering.*

How shall I unwind me from the spool of you?
Too well, we let our privacies untangle. Do
angels bless such shabby vows? Our crimson bed,
far wide for treaty reaps the fruit of blame. Untold,

my hands are ashen as the lights of Mercury
and red as every darling sin. You kiss my thigh
from habit only when we name the birds and beasts:
woman, serpent, traitor-fish, *acrobat me?*—

Take that rib and shove it where it hasn't seen.
Your neck is fig-thistle, your groin, a could have been,
but wasn't. Clever God, He made an incense of
your musk—the burdens of appeal, *unfortunate us.*

Dry Seasons

The blanched dunes and disembodied wells
sing cruel, *soft*, then bright as stones.
I failed you as a cloud would fail.
So clumsy and cumulo-nimbic of me—
I gave you grief, not empathy.

You said my eyes were always black. I looked away,
and then—you were not there. You bribed the dogs
with candy not to tell. For forty days,
I sniffed your shirts and your cigars.
I kissed the razor, I tried to forge a scar,

and then I followed the shrug of your footsteps here.
I called out *darling* but no one turned to see.
Is it breath, your name under the sear
of this sun that haunts me? I frighten as a maiden's hand,
set steady to pluck a rattler from its sand.

If I should rub Sahara into my skin tonight until
it smarts and I know better, then I will sleep.
Come. *Home.* I am old from bending at your trail.
The crumbs you dropped are stale and I am tired,
having sifted the grain of such flesh from my desire.

Ararat

Even as he sleeps, I hear
the snore of my own drowsy longings.
It is a number of tiny deaths,
this dilemma of belonging

to someone like him
to whom it did not matter who he wed.
And tell me what is worse,
being married or being dead?

I built a boat, I called it our bed,
and I shared *ors*
and *ifs* with him until we creaked.
He says he loves me more

each day. Forget it. He loves no one
but himself, and even then, only some
of the time. It's been raining forty days at least?
More like seven damn

years. I am wet and tired as ugly wool,
the unicorns have bailed,
and the stupid dove's got a nosegay
of stinkweed in her beak. I did not fail

him so badly. Indeed, the rainbow lacked
a stripe or two, impaired
as the both of us (but mostly, it was him,
who did not mind the stench of a pair

of everything turning sour
in the drawers and in the sockets).
There is nowhere to go but down,
and Honey, I can't swim. My pockets

bulge with animals and want.
That I am not sunken is a miracle,
for ours is a teeming, a heavy vessel,
called frigate of folly, or ferry of debacle.

Apple Magic

Is it the drip-heavy sweetness of fruit on your fingers,
the six A.M. curl and reach towards birthing sky?
Yes, it is the sweetness of this apple and you are alive—
your teeth buried in pulp and skin, in the biting, the chewing,
as if on me you're going down. The belly of the fruit is yours,
was always.

Thank God for all of this, for the beginning
when we all arose from tricks with clay,
for the unperfected dumb and bumbling Adam
who wept as he fell, or for Johnny Appleseed
who planted row after row singing *Oh
the Lord is good to me.*

Now we eat and drink, go forth to multiply,
together two and two, we are the continent and the sea,
a pair of Arks on Ararat, the south pole rising in the north.

Let the apple trees keep their uneven,
sympathetic rows, and draw me to your lap.
The days ahead will wait as we return
to the bounty of unkempt sheets,
a warm and reverent orchard we shall raise.

Elegy

My body lifted from the fold of yours
    in a distorted dream:
I was the smoke you suffered in a fire,
    as well the scald of relief
when fume and flame rose off dismissing
    broken chairs and burst balloons.
You were near perfect under me,
    exact as a measuring cup or spoon.

There is nothing left to say except
    I'm sorry Dear, I failed.
I blessed you—or, I tried—as if a martyr's tooth.
    Like that I nailed
my wrists against your errant, ornate cross,
    then cried up *it is finished*.
Now I am an empty tomb, stone-numb
    where your mouth ever touched—

How little I have learned, all told.
    Tonight, your breath an integer
lost in the factoring, or a rusty abacus
    I cannot figure.
You, the scroll of Torah waiting
    on the nightstand to be read,
as I ponder missing comforts—
    porridge, socks, or wedding beds.

Sarah-Song

Laughter—the grief of happiness
in a tinny voice, and though you weep less
than you smile these days, your old woman heart
is confused as any altar in the desert,

searching out the east when there is none,
and the fact of *how could this be?*, when one
can never ask such things of God.
How *can't* this be? Indeed, the child

you carried is not miracle, the Infinite
can manage anything, even this infant
from a carved out womb.
And what he will become

the angels cannot tell: is it flesh or fire?,
the princely intricate of his bones, or desire
burning at his temples like a sanctuary bell?—
Mother, all who see this marvel joy as well.

The Furnace

I have tried you in the furnace of affection.

I am looking through a window
    and there is no glass,
and you fumble again.
    It is always like this—
you, dancing the dance of the scorched,
    the somewhat singed,
with brightly vague non-flammables
    wrapped around your head.

Uncomfortably, we slip off
    the undershirts and socks,
and if I let you lay on top of me,
    it is only sex which touches sex.
I keep all dear embraces for myself,
    else I burn in your Gehenna. I must.
Otherwise, I am near comfortless,
    sorry and undressed

as Eve with nowhere in the room
    to turn for shade. Granted,
all vows are terminable, even these,
    yet is this all we promised?—
Well, no. But in the end, every saint
    will have to die, and so we
do it with the light on, always.
    It is coldest that way.

The World to Come

December is the month of nativity,
of Mary's milk and perfect embryos,
of Magi traveling far on asses to bring gifts.
The cross seems promising so far away,
prismatic beyond its splinters,

as in Wisconsin, when, driving
through the county grounds at midnight,
he turns off the headlights of the car
to show me the luster of dry snow
under moonlight, and all is calm.

Indeed there are storms in winter,
and for every birth we celebrate,
there is a corollary which holds
that breathing is a temporary state,
and death, being ever natural,

is as white as a virgin birth
or any showing of grace, made whiter
in its stillness. The gravity of snow
is a deepening glaze, and the wintry promise of the wind
that you will shiver, and shiver again, so be prepared—

but I am so near sleep this night and none
of this occurs to me. Because I am naïve,
my version of the Christmas king will live
at least a hundred happy years, dying in his sleep
as he dreams rams and ewes,

and money never changes hands. Were this truly so,
I could easily believe in a world to come
worthy of the name Paradise,
a heaven that's for sweethearts, sons and snow,
and not for God with all his funny angels, laughing.

The Faster's Prayer

Yesterday I thought I heard Him in
my kitchen measuring flour to bake a loaf
of Bread of Life—

wasn't I surprised to see the rats
had learned such mysteries of God, and from
the garbage they were snickering failure
as they blessed my host.

Eve at Noon

So you return to God, palming
a piece of fruit so luscious it seems
to have made itself from mud, nothing
else, so perfect you have no idea

it grew from a cleft-seed, slantwise
at the river of cold and blue,
where the apple is inconsequential.

So you go empty-handed as a bird
having flown that same river, a bird
who dove into it, came up hungry.

Would you then remember to remake
yourself from mosses and a kiss of clay?
Would you live for that?

The Apostate's Creed

the present of that world has passed away

I believe in God, but
he was someone else's father
long and far ago.

And I believe God had a son,
born under the half-shadow of him.
It was disaster, the bad and unwise star,
his better parts worse for the wear.

He suffered under Venus' ashen light.
He climbed up a tree to reveal himself.
He waited there as I have waited many times.
He died and that was that.

I believe in the Spirit, but the Spirit is sad.
Whatever will satisfy the cobwebbed,
crooked angels, always at the altar of us,
beflowered, with ragged hands?

Epiphany

There will always be a sign:
I am naked under the stars,
which means I am guilty of something.

It is January cold, and
I am here because you said so,
I cannot help it. These,

the only clues our nights have left,
the desert carrying on and on,
while a violin laments the secret life of me.

This gold-gilt box is for the child,
I have signed both our names.
If my posture for prayer seems

irreverent, then you are too frail
and I should kiss your buttons
and your bones, ever as delicate

as any precise moment of longing—
I tremble as a sinking leaf, and you,
my covenant, I take you everywhere with me.

Jonah

Now I think I understand:
you were a clean wall
and these menacing hands
have stained you with prints
from my sweaty glands.

You ran quite far and almost
got away. But I set
fire to your ghost,
and the sweet, sick haze
of that burning rose

has found you out.
You hid yourself
in the stout
bow of a schooner,
where you fought

visions of me with sticks,
swiping the air
in violent strikes.
But I survived,
and I stand solid, fixed

by tendons in my knotty womb.
It is your final gift
to me: this room
where I shall bleed and knit,
as spinsters do.

God

I blame you for most of this—the evidence
of nothing much my pillow offers, alibis
of goose-down, tears at three A.M., the snow-squall cries
my spirit throats, concluding you make no damn sense

at all, to most of us, *to me.* Your face is under
gauze and ever at a distance. Other sheep
may bleat your countenance in full, but I perceive
just flutters of an eyelash, or the lead and usher

of a temporary tongue. If heaven is
as supple, blue, and otherwise as blizzard ice,
then why not me? Unmask the seraphim—they brood

as I do—painlessly, often with moans of praise
to pass the hours. And the dead stay dead. Like me, wise
to nothing tangible, not body, neither blood.

The Feast of the Transfiguration

A light rain, and slight
chill in the air— only *that*,
the unquiet of not quite cold
but almost, and growing colder.

He is on my mind again,
but the stay is brief enough
that I might try to forget him
as I would try to forget

the yet awkward hands
of a maladroit lover,
or a long, a bad night,
of which there have been too many.

Beloved, the soap still bears
the imprint of your thumbs,
and my sheets, the contours
of whatever murmurs you once dreamed.

Upon which bright mountain
will I turn pale before such ravished eyes?
Will I sweeten as new wine
in the rite of the remade?

Perhaps, but I have eaten bitter decades up
already, just to choke on what is
something more divine than grief,
having swallowed the glories such suffering brings.

Wednesday, Ash

Nothing of me will survive.
This body that I wear will die
and my mouth—nevermind its loveliness—
is set to shut itself into a sorrow the size

of restlessness and lack.
The lips go too. They slack
at the corners crying *no, no*
but still they go. They do not talk back.

And then for every finger I have counted on—
so many times—there is a going, and a gone.
They leave to rest in pieces with once sad and pretty
    hands of grief
waiting for an Easter dawn

(which no one hears approaching when they're buried
    underneath the ground).
And my feet cannot quit thinking quickstep, swing, the sound
of toe taps or a waltz. *Hush.* No dancing for the dead.
The ball is done. The slipper? *Nowhere to be found.*

And my belly, full or no is quiet.
Then it will feast as a ghost feasts—on nothing, a diet
of sediment, sleep, a lily or two.
I shall not fuss, I shall not make riot

or rivalry any, *any* more. The eyes are vacant, tenantless,
for they have been plucked out. Relentless
death, you have withered shut my heart
like an old rose closing, pungent and motionless

in the closet of the rats and of the bones. Everything I am is dust,
or shadows of it, clay unkissed.
Having died in the desert, I do not come back.
Having died in the desert, it is the drought I miss.

How can that *be*? Nothing, nothing of us survives.
Every inch of us will die,
and not a thing that God can do will stop it.
Even Christ, the very self of God was crucified

and dead three days, entombed.
Angels wept as little children, women loomed
about His bloody, broken body swaddled in a shroud.
And then—He rose. Like Lazarus or bread, or any bright moon

which lifts as thunder over mountaintops and homes.
Like that, my God—save me, save me from the groan
and creak of a coffin's rusty hinge
and resurrect us all, one by one—

all the bodies that no longer breathe or move,
and every soul that reaches but cannot grasp the thing it loves.
Save us to a grace we cannot ever hope to understand,
such that in our dyings—behold—*somehow?*—we live.

Whispers of the Kingdom

When everything she touched
seemed to turn up paper or pain
she forged a new self
from tufts of moss and the inaugural ash
found at the stations of the cross, saying
anything that is too much me,
I must strip away.

How lucky then, for her hands.
They learned to knit without needles
or yarn, and in the distance
between being lost and being saved,
she fashioned for herself an invisible shawl
resembling feathers, and it fit around her
just well enough that when offered a drink

from the fugitive cup of all things living and dead
she flew up above it, to the crossbeams
and the lamps, to nest and to hide
as if a hermit mockingbird, having no part
of our troubles and making no sense
to our sadness, and singing, always

singing *nearer to thee.*
Grace, I will watch her with wonder from below,
summing carefully each of the marigold praises
to tumble from the seam of such a woman's lip,
and tending her every need as if she were me.
As if she were me.

The Dance of Salome

Put on your quickest pearls and wear
    that castanety sort of grin
that plays so well on foreign films,
    or cruel lips of pretty girls.
Then lift your chin to sweep the arch
    and architecture of your curls
to an etiquette of balconies toasting coffee pots
    with Sapphire Gin.
Darling, say good evening to the refrigerator
    and the bed—
it is better to be dancing than be dead.

Call the doctor up, and tell him
    he's no longer any use.
You're cured of anything he could invent,
    with nothing he could trim
away you do not need. You are intact,
    a perfect, luscious gem
whose heart is not accessory to wear
    as purses or papoose.
You are body, wholly body, *holy body*
    as it has been said—
tell everyone how better to be dancing than be dead!

If your beau does not quite suit you,
    turn him in for someone else
and that was merely one good hour wasted,
    time enough to test
the timbre of his flesh against the willow
    of your thighs, at best
a gauge against the Him whose lack you suffer

only in your self.
And when you fear the colors of that terror
    in your dizzy head—
remember: *far better to be dancing than be dead.*

Now dance me into frenzy, into madness,
    into deaf and dumb.
Swing it like your daddy's grief
    you didn't marry Mister Right,
or Father Mike who heard you tell too many times
    of suspect nights
you couldn't quite recall but felt safe-sure
    that you'd been bad. My plum,
my dancing, drizzling fruitcake sweet as any piece
    that can be had—
better for you to dance than be dead.

Lest your mother weep for nothing,
    wear your hair in droopy locks
and flirt the room as if you were not born
    for any other strut.
Your skirt hiked up to Neverland,
    wear daisies at your breast and put
the bones of John the Baptist
    in your garter and your box.
Undo the top three buttons of your blouse
    and leave the rest unsaid,
for it is better to be dancing than be dead.

Passiontide

It always hurts to be this clean:
the ache and bend of water over me,
but I go back again,
each time, intinctured and wafer thin
as a host, if indeed I am what I eat.

Why have you covered my face?
I lost my path this way
before, at Eastertime,
and I was neither sanctified
nor saved. Is there no place

on earth for me? This Lent I wear a choir's
worth of crowns I've shaped from wire,
bone, and kindling twigs—
am I queen of something fig,
or something fire?

The Last of All Suppers

It is bone-cold the night of all betrayed,
as shadows in the shape of thieves play
against the linens of the tent—quiet, odd
figures moving as fingers over old wood,
searching for splinters. The sound
of money changing hands,
as doves coo *fool, fool* from rafter nests.
A rustling noise, swift
as paradise, then it is a falter of a scream,
firestarter, perhaps, or the seam
of someone's papyric arms beginning to unravel:
Drink it. This is neither me nor miracle.
Hide him in the quiet marrow of your bed
where dozens eat no poetry and Jesus weeps no bread.

Glory Be

last night I imagined
god was a woman god
and when I prayed
it was   *mother thank you*
for the day just past
and   *mother thank you*
for the day to come and
mother keep me safe another
night, unbroken and preserved
like a favorite doll

but something is not true
in that   if god were woman-
flesh she would not just say
take and eat   it would be *take*
and eat more   and we would know it
in the faces of those stodgy ministers
who never seem to smile
for their faces would be marvelous
from chin to brow as they
grinned   *lord*
do you look beautiful in red.

Thursday

At the midnight of our trouble,
there are signs in the moon and in the stars.
He will not say that he belongs to me,
and still I bend to wash his feet.

Evanescent grace, you vanish as a vapor
does, or love in open air. I am helpless
under him and begging reconciliation bodywise,
the onset of my mouth against his thighs.

And when and if he touches me, I feel treasure
to him, the luxury of centuries to come,
forever and for good, the gentle fall of weather
over us, something borrowed, blue, or better.

Someday this will end, all say.
I consecrate the oils and strip the altar bare.
Tomorrow we shall have no meat—
darling my body, *take and eat.*

Lullaby for a Good Friday

What is it like to be nailed to a tree?
They beat your face until it was
No more a face. Catastrophe
Becomes you, Christ. Amid the buzz

Of fools and faith, it is another
Good one wasted on ourselves.
Your retinue wears black, your mother
Weeps, and Joseph builds a shelf.

Did you pray for steady hands,
A room of your own to go and to think,
A place to hide from fishermen,
A heart of coal, another drink?

The weight of day lies on your shoulders.
How dark these hours from noon to three.
Forget the crucifix and boulder—
Close your eyes and fall asleep.

Post-Communion Striptease

for L—

Imagine me elsewhere and kneeling—
however do I survive among such textures
of salvation and praise, feeling

in degrees the stern glimmer of the chalice
where I am reflected in abstract,
an image of convexity and some malice

I've kept quiet on? I have lover's knees
and the mouth of an undiscovered
artist. Where do I belong among these

saved? If I tease my hands into reverence,
they might stay that way for good— alas,
we feed on grace with bitter condiments,

and this supper never satisfies. Should it?
I look ridiculous in dinner dress, clothed
in the humilities of well-stitched vestments

and sensible shoes. If the costume
of repentance is a new self, perfectly pressed,
then I am weary of my Sunday suit.

If I undo these buttons on the cassock of remorse,
you'll see I do not grieve for much I've done,
as well as I've forgotten my brassiere. And the farce

of wearing these impoverished stockings of devotion
is only bearable with garter snaps, half fastened.
What do I have underneath this robe? Confusion,

and the ghost of every fingerprint that's confessed
to my thighs, so much that aches to be revealed,
my ultimate wish— to be safe and undressed

at once and for good, to be uncovered without fear, bare
as a winter elm, a heart exposed yet loved
despite itself. Then, if I fall, having snared

my feet in the hems of my nakedness, I claim
whatever right deserves the maladroit:
to land between God blessed and God damned.

Easter

and the Christians are at it again,
raising the dead, weaving what's left of the fin
folds of the ichthys into fish-nets
and unburial shrouds, having fits
of praise and panic near the empty tomb.
And the early rooster, so proud of his comb
this morning, is all cock and crowing
risen, risen, to the sun, half-glowing
in the revenant mist of miracles
and rolled-away stones, the debacle
of any needy flesh, leavened as bread.
Your king was not quite dead,
He was only napping.
So feast, you believing souls, on bing
cherries and all the vibrant eggs
you can gather, scratch *alleluia* into your legs
with the slivers of the splintered
cross, give every bloody grief to winter
and her blizzard frown,
your Christ has sprung up and grown
new buds as a dogwood might,
or the eclipsed moon, fresh light.
And though I joy to think
that death is not so vicious as that low, blank
whistle of a breath I thought that it would be—
what god has risen me?

Calvary

I had nearly forgotten those footsteps
which led to the brow of that merciless hill
where we met, night after dreary night,
wearing nothing but the doze of our sleepy skins,
and waiting for sunlight, the flicker of doves—

but last night I dreamt of Magdalene's scarves.
There were holes where her fingers had troubled them bare,
and I sniffed them as I would inhale any sad thing
or sacrifice, wrapping them deep around my prayers.
They smelled of violins and myrrh.

He is not here. Where did it go, my grief, my grief?
Once you loved me on a hillside. I was pretty
and tender as silence. Some things I knew well enough:
first you love and then you lose.
I had no idea there was nothing more.

Tongues of Fire

This is what's become of us: I am
confused by mourning, and he is the sun
that goes to sleep on top of me, undone
by moonrise. Lover, all I speak is iambs

and slant rhyme. That devil lamb
of light called hope is sacrificed and none
too pleased with having lost its bleat. The stone
has rolled away but God's not gone and damn

it, I'm no fan of the weather here, it rains
too often, bones of doves and angel down
until the ground stains red with sighs and blood.

It is wet and cold. Will you explain
again the why of all there is and how
he caught me in the act, discovering God?

Sex among the Christians

Lean into me as a steeple might
and I will turn your flesh to food
as stars call shepherds to our room
on any Bethlehemic night.

Kiss as if you were a Jew,
a crucifix to whet your thighs.
Some April morning you will rise—
oh Christ was once a man like you.

Resurrection Hill

I looked up to the rumble of the clouds,
and everything opened as the sky
fell inches from my face and I fought
the long fire with my hands, harps
playing of their own accord.

They staggered up from ribs of stone and soil,
my first husband, and wives of many simple men,
urchins, thrones, mothers of us all. They seemed blanker
than when first they left, as if Heaven were a clinic,
and they were cured.

Then it was you, strange and fragile you, rubbing
the sleep from your eyes and stretching your back,
as the earth rattled like a satisfied woman,
and the moon shining not so brightly above—

I wept as I had not cried in ten thousand years,
the philharmonic angels strumming at my sobs.
You were yet cold, but still I threw my arms to you,
taking years to remap the province of your body.

How far away they seem, each of those nights
that I slept with my body curled into the absence of yours,
dreaming the lullaby of your tepid wheeze
and drowning in that queasy, blue sea of loss.

Evensong

Every night, it is one drunken orbit after another,
and the moon makes its rounds about the sky
as I kneel outside the garden turning stones
in time with serpents and figs.

Dizzy and cold, the stars are wearing veils of grief
and weeping as if over me.

Under such a sky the only sense I have of myself
is senselessness—the indiscriminate aching
in the spoon of my neck which comes
like noise in the night, quick
and hysterical, the breaking up of things
that should not be so fragile.

When I was a child, I played like a child
I dressed like a child, I ate like a child,
I cried like a child, I worried as a child worries
over sudden things, the fall of nighttime skies
or Jesus with his very eyes on me.

Dim mirror above, reflect more brightly upon us all.
From here, I see nothing but myself
and the face of me is trembling.

Untilling

This garden seems to grow
whether I want it to or no,
and then—it vanishes.

Where did I leave it last?
Every sprig of hope I plant
turns wilty in my palm,

the itch of bloom and thorn.
And you, my serpent, ruminant worm,
have eaten through the fruit

and pleaded deaf and dumb.
I've scored each acre with these thumbs,
sowing for the truth,

but Christ, for all I know
was just a carpenter, mistletoe
besides and cross to bear.

Still, I cultivate.
As if I could resuscitate
my fig and apple faith.

Eve, Ever After

for Axel

First it is a kiss, and then that strange twine
of silence knotting the twin of your lips into mine,
the stench of far-ripe apples on our breaths.
In lieu of lambs, I give my breasts

as offering to burn in your desire or your hands.
Let it come to me quickly, this flame while you empty the land
of its figs as the bewildering, intricate eye of God
frowns over our naked bodies as if they already understood

each other. I am hazy and vulnerable tonight, floating as a jellyfish
in shallow tide, me, your dearly awkward bobber flush
with as much grace as can muster the soon to be set
to the beach. I am your missing rib, yet significant,

that simple bone withdrawn or lost, regained.
This is hardly Eden, now a ghost of it, the veined
head of a serpent lingering at my chin
and hissing futile psalms about Jerusalem.

I will die someday. But tonight, you lace
yourself in me again, teaching me the language of this place.
Then we build a bed from Tree of Knowledge wood.
We christen it Heaven, and stay there for good.

Equinox

Everywhere I look is something new to grieve:
the autumnal groans of retributing leaves,
the casualty of early fall retiring into winter.
So many years have left this September
with peahens sobbing *going, gone.*

I am not in pain, I am in sadness. It is
a disheveled cauldron of a bed, this shiftless
winter rest whose coming I taste by the flavor of the wind
turning tin on my tongue when the bruised reed bends,
and girls stitch immortelles upon their sleeves.

The God who I only know by His goings
leaves for good, His last, His fatal showing,
His *Rest in Peace.* It is the Law of Diminishing Returns.
The heart has finally approached that which it yearns,
or yearns to yearn at least, and then—it disappears

as the trees in winter heaving traitor to the sun
burning cold, then coldest on December dawns
and Christmas is just another day of feasting.
What makes me weak? So many—*many*—things.
Christ, how far the throne of heaven seems.

Thirty-Three

If the martyr is made when the breaking heart breaks open,
and one holds in the crib of her palm the ghost
of something as singular as last night's argument,
then what was mystery is worse—the advent of the end.

They sleep in the sea of a bed, blue as breath,
the tangle of needle-net holding them close.
And if they dance, it is like lanterns on a lake,
as nothing lasts for very long, so frail, those passive vessels.

Imagine the elemental glow and a city of stars still forming,
the work in progress of heaven like the swirl of color
in a vanity rose: where one shade ends the other
may begin, or not, its own red.

She scowls her lover's scowl. When Christ comes
down from the mountain, he marches to Jerusalem unaware.
This is how the dead get by, and the dying make due:
like anyone, they are preserved with such affection
as to disenchant their grief.

Rib

I frown because you frustrate me,
your wooly, muffled voice, and the dishes
that will not do themselves.

I have traded word for weary word
with you and come up short so many sentences,
that I am broke from paying attention.

Maybe I have treated you badly.
I am sorry if I have treated you badly,
but other men have worn me out,

and I no longer make love, it will not last.
So if I linger at the arcs of your chest,
we shall call it mere tenderness, or homecoming.

And if I happen to write sonnets in the honor of us,
I will not drown you in burdens of marigolds,
rather clay, a kiss or two, some serpents looking on.

I am near useless here, and if I cross myself,
it is only because I am that lost,
with nothing left to do for my hands.

Heaven

To live well under this dark shadow,
it takes deep breathing and a resolution,
for here it is monstrous cold,

and the wind has teeth as large as testament.
I wrap a sweater around the sleeve
of my soul, and night after night,

I sit and I stare at pumpkins, at the moon,
at roses falling short of themselves.
They are thorn and mere bloom,

and I no longer know if they are beautiful,
just as I no longer know if I am beautiful,
and whether I am or I am not, I do not know

if it matters, if it ever did. *Nevermind.*
I am still as uncertain, or at least just as chill
as this gray sky above, and that one cold hope

success, below, and this unsavory room
of waning passions in between.
I wanted to make music or love,

and having the talents for neither, I settled on both.
Do you see these scars?
They bear the teethmarks of the angels.

Naked in the Garden

As over all things, God is over me—
impersonally, a subtle body stilling me
to stone, the flood and plague of your voice.

What is so impossible about desire?
Angels who have trimmed their wings
cannot sing choruses to higher thrones.

When I cross myself, it is to predispose
my sanctity. I leave bed-making to you.
The vapor of my breath

against your chest, and I shall only rise
to wash my hands. I am sweaty and profuse,
savage as fire. Everything I never said

trails from your beard as filament,
indefinite and thin. I am cold from regret.
On Sunday you kissed me in the statuary.

The cobbled face of Jesus seemed
to sag a little when I stood too close.
Me without a cover for my head.

Concerning the Ends of Us

After Jonathon Edwards

It's the devil in me, I suppose,
or the damsel slope of my aristocratic nose
or the earthquakes coming of my every prayer
to rumble and throb at the epicenter of all doubt, but year

after year I make these promises:
I will be a Good Enough, says
me, I will be kind to children,
and slack off the booze and act with Christian

fortitude all times, all ways. Damn if I don't go curly trying.
Attempts aside, forget it. I'm dying
of a malady named *egocitosis*,
and you are too—the self shifts

shimmy like a snake into the corners
sanctified as *soul*. And it lingers
there, and multiplies like cancer or a hutch
of Easter rabbits. The heart, which

isn't immune to anything, turns numb to all
others, dumb as the muscle that it is, and Hell
is where the sickest of us go to colonize
as lepers far away from Heaven's well. If I

know this, it's because I've seen it in a dream.
God, who from the earth seems
so regal to us, austere
as Solomon, doesn't care

where we wind up in the end.
It's not that He's no good. Rather, God depends
on nothing save but God. And we are zero added
but the glory of God's own bad-

assed idea to call us made. Still, we barter with the Him
each day, begging *Sir, the hem*
of your garment and I will be fit
to be whole, or close to it

at least—as if by this God's joy is secure.
Not that there isn't hope, of course. The sure
way to paradise is turn right at the tree
and keep your eyes shut up like the knees

of a virgin lest the luscious fruit be tempting.
Then, it's not called sinning,
it's called getting by. And if we do it just so,
when we die our maker calls us to the throne

and we shall sit there eternities long
as jesters in the courts of a king
who is far independent of us. And the soul
we keep pristine as sculptor's ice is well,

and our spirits ever in the eyesights of the Father,
whose cataract gaze is like bruises left by water.

Kenosis

a great disturbance came to pass among the jars
—from a Valentinian gospel

It is a paschal sort of grief,
as in jelly, quivering,
this body that I bleed away,
the bravery of emptying.

I am a broken vessel, Lord—
rubble where a soul should be,
this body that I bleed away
for heaven's sake, or sympathy's,

and wreckage never to be found.
None but you will ever see
the body I have bled away,
as Isaac as an offering.

I trim myself, a sacrifice
of prunes and pearls, a reliquary
of a body, bled away,
the patron of debility.

Eventide

The clouds seem drawn towards the sun
as if by magnets and the strangeness
of the darkening sky,

or the shape of it.
I am stumbling, searching
for safety's sake, another bed.

This fog prefers my neck tonight.
Though I may dream of elephants
oceans away, and other things,

it is the wedding ring I lost,
a gradient wind and the chill
of any unexpected summer storm.

As in a Eucharist, so much is mystery:
the furrow in your gaze,
the tired, the saline face of grief.

The Coming

When apple-birds have drowned themselves in milk,
the old bones take it well. They gather smoke
to ink the mountainsides with letters of
regret. And when the moon burns through its orbit,
men take cover in cramped rooms, while all
the dead begin to roil within the ground.
And as He comes, the night completes itself.
The end arrives as if a telegram,
in series, inconsolably. And if
they wish to suckle the Messiah's breast,
it is too late, He's dry. Look to the stars—
a trumpet and a train conclude the sky.

When the Kingdom Comes

Your mother is not your mother,
she is something else, a bird nesting in the heart
of a hollowed out tree, a saint whose skin is cool
and soft as apple-flesh, the will of God.

And your brothers are not your brothers,
they are the ash that is all of us,
scattered in its periphery,
unfortunate multitude.

Your sister, your lover, your friend
none of these are yours.
The stone belongs only to the river
which bled it smooth.

What you call your face, that canvas of mercy
which smiles with grief at even November's
drizzle and chill, is the face of someone else,
someone to come, *good tidings*,

the Christ child in a stable,
cooing as Mary tends such tiny hands.
It is her face that seems so familiar,
the answer to everything whetting the tip of your tongue.

The hairs on your head, they belong only
to themselves, and when they are done
with such a manner of belonging,
they offer themselves to stars

which outnumber them galacticly.
Everything you think is yours is not.
A father had two sons, and one of them
was heavy with desire. Friend—what's lost is found,

forever. You will wear the very best robe.
You will wear rings on every finger
of each hand. And they are not your hands.
They are God's hands,

and She formed you with them Herself
turning tricks with clay until finally
the sand sang *alleluia,* and it was good.
These hands, She will hold like treasure

all the way to Paradise, where under the glimmer of the moon
and the spark of light that fuels every prayer,
She keeps her family. And we will all be there.
And we will all *be.*

Paradise

This bridge of moon on bended knee above us
keening twilight and the snake that is
your tongue has taught itself to sing, to sing.

My hand so heavy with your hand, your eyes
brimmed curve to crease with grief, and you chant
Bread will be the body of a king,

someday. With a voice like every nectarine,
so lovely and so bruised, how I am tempted
to you, famished as a rite of spring

mid-winter underneath the tricky snow,
broom-cold, tripping fig over foot, husky
and nervous as the glassy oxen, staggering.

Remember, I am but a rib. I curve
into your spine and wrap about your heart,
fleshless as marrow, your vitreous darling.

PHOTO BY BOB KINNEY

ABOUT THE AUTHOR

Jill Alexander Essbaum was born in southeast Texas in 1971. Educated at the University of Houston, the University of Texas, and the Episcopal Theological Seminary of the Southwest, her poetry has appeared in both local and national journals, including *Artful Dodge, Borderlands, Rattle,* and the *Texas Observer.* She lives in Austin with her husband, Axel.

LIBRARY OF CONGRESS CATALOGING-IN-PUBLICATION DATA

Essbaum, Jill Alexander.
Heaven / Jill Alexander Essbaum.
    p. cm. — (Middlebury/Bread Loaf book)
"The Katharine Bakeless Nason literary publication prizes."
    ISBN 1–58465–045–1 (alk. paper) — ISBN 1–58465–046–x (pbk. : alk. paper)
    I. Title. II. Series.
    PS3555.S66 H43 2000
    811'.6—dc21   00–008924

POETR

In elegant , and rebel-
lious to question der Essbaum retells
the Biblical story and explores the meaning of love through the
eyes of an archetypal Eve. Her poems speak of unsure faith, the theology
of doubt, and the uncertainty of anything divine, placed against a back-
ground of skeptical yet fervent hope that God *is*, despite such disbelief.

"Only the best writers put us right at the site of myth and thus assert, for us,
our right to be part of the beginning and end of any world, any heaven.
That Jill Alexander Essbaum does it so quietly, so delicately, and puts her-
self, and us, at the center of Heaven *itself* leads me only to envy. For how
else can one convincingly transcend the domestic? There is simply no self-
congratulation in these poems. Just a graceful, magical way of taking one-
self—and one's bare uncertainties—for granted."
—Agha Shahid Ali, Judge

"The poems of *Heaven* are fabulously forged in the furnace of passionate
spirit—they rise, still molten, into our sight. Jill Alexander Essbaum writes
with a rare lyrical exactitude, fusing religious iconography with her own
human journey so all the elements—spiritual, physical, intellectual—are
reinvented, recharged. For an immediate classic, try 'When the Kingdom
Comes.' There's an organic, startling music here, and the gift of a brilliant
heart."
—Naomi Shihab Nye

Recipient of an M.A. from the University of Texas and candidate for an
M.A.R. from Episcopal Theological Seminary of the Southwest, **Jill Alexan-
der Essbaum** lives and works in Austin, Texas. Her poetry has appeared in
many journals, including *Artful Dodge*, *Borderlands*, and the *Texas Observer.*

Bread Loaf Writers' Conference
Middlebury College Press

PUBLISHED BY UNIVERSITY PRESS OF NEW ENGLAND

HANOVER AND LONDON

www.upne.com

COVER ILLUSTRATION: Phillip Ratner, sculptor,
Eve and Serpent. Collection of the Dennis and
Phillip Ratner Museum.
www.ratnermuseum.com

ISBN 1–58465–046–X

90000

9 781584 650461